D1452578

# BIG-HEARTED
# LEADERSHIP

# BIG-HEARTED LEADERSHIP

## FIVE KEYS TO CREATE SUCCESS THROUGH COMPASSION

### DONN SORENSEN
#### WITH VAUGHN KOHLER

WISE
CREATIVE + PUBLISHING
*Ink*

Print ISBN: 978-1-63489-031-1
eISBN: 978-1-63489-032-8

Library of Congress Catalog Number: 2016932169

Printed in the USA
First Printing: 2016

20   19   18   17   16          5   4   3   2   1

Cover and interior design by James Monroe Design, LLC.

Wise Ink, Inc.
837 Glenwood Avenue
Minneapolis, Minnesota  55405

wiseinkpub.com
To order, visit itascabooks.com or call 1-800-901-3480.
Reseller discounts available.

This book is dedicated to the sisters, coworkers, and physicians of Mercy Health who make the lives of others' their life's work.

You have made my life richer and more meaningful.

# Contents

CHAPTER ONE:
Give Your People a Structure They Can Lean On
15

CHAPTER TWO:
Be "Here" and "With"
33

CHAPTER THREE:
Be Generous in Your Genuineness
51

CHAPTER FOUR:
Possess (and Pass On) Enduring Enthusiasm
67

# Foreword

Donn Sorensen is a blond-haired, blue-eyed Scandinavian man from Rochester, Minnesota. I am an African-American woman from East St. Louis, Illinois. Some might wonder how we hit it off so well, but the truth is, we've got my favorite thing in the world in common: running.

Donn is a big guy. If you didn't know any better, you would assume he went to college on a football scholarship. Not so; he ran track and field. Since we share this bond, Donn and I both know that to be a good runner, you have to have solid form. You have to set a training schedule and stick to it, using the right techniques to improve your speed and endurance. And, of course, it never hurts to be born with natural athleticism. It always helps to have speed in your genes.

But there's something else that makes a good runner. Olympic-level runners—well, really all elite athletes—have it in spades. It's *desire.* Those who have succeeded on the highest stages have all had that one quality in common: they wanted to win. A lot. When it came to winning, *they cared.* Donn's approach to leadership is the same as an elite runner's approach to a big race.

Donn has been serving as an executive in the medical-management industry for more than three decades. As a leader, he's had a great run. He's helped different organizations overcome significant challenges, and he's spearheaded a number of charitable and philanthropic efforts. He's got great form and technique. Fundamentally, Donn is a very effective leader. He exudes excellence. He's a big-picture guy who also cares about the details. He has a strong personality and is also approachable. He's a fun guy, but also knows when it's time to get down to business. He commands respect, but he also gives it. You know the Golden Rule, "Do unto others as you'd have them do unto you"? Donn doesn't ask anyone to do anything that he doesn't do himself. He embodies leadership, and he knows how to exercise it.

But above all, Donn cares. In fact, as he'll tell you again and again, there are things you might be able to criticize about him, but you can never say that he doesn't care. He cares a lot. He cares about the success of the organization he serves (even a casual observer can see that he works tirelessly). He cares about the community in which he lives (he's super active in charitable organizations; that's how we met originally, as he was helping me with my foundation). Bottom line: he cares about people. (I think that's why he's so excited to be the president of Mercy East Region—an organization whose doctors and staff help thousands of people every day.)

Spend just a little time with Donn, and you won't be surprised that this book is titled Big-Hearted Leadership. He does have a big heart. He shows it often; whether he's smiling, laughing, or giving out hugs. But you'll never be tempted to think he's all about warm fuzzies and not action and results. With a résumé and work history that ranks among the best, Donn's career speaks for itself.

I'm excited and honored to recommend Big-Hearted Leadership to you. It'll give you a basic form and technique for effective leadership. And it'll inspire you to be a Big-Hearted Leader yourself. It'll inspire you to care—about success and about people.

**–Jackie Joyner-Kersee**

Founder, Jackie Joyner-Kersee Foundation
Three-time gold medal award–winning Olympian
Called "World's Greatest Female Athlete" by Sports Illustrated

# 2nd Foreword

IN MY THIRTY-THREE YEARS OF SERVING AS AN EXECutive with the Boeing Company, I've been exposed to a lot of management and manufacturing philosophies, methods, and processes. I've learned what works best and what doesn't work at all. One systematic method I learned later in my career that stands out in my experience—and it's one I continue to advise companies and organizations to implement now that I'm a full-time consultant—is called LEAN manufacturing or production. Or simply: a LEAN program.

In layman's terms, LEAN is a system originally embraced by Toyota of Japan to improve quality, performance, and employee engagement. The Japanese culture is known for its simplicity and conservation, so it's no surprise that the LEAN program is based on simplifying processes and operations and minimizing waste.

But it goes beyond that. The Boeing Company, the largest aerospace company in the world, is (in my opinion at least) the greatest practitioner and innovator of LEAN. After more than three decades of working for Boeing, I witnessed firsthand how LEAN achieves the seemingly impossible. Whether it was by establishing uniform, repeatable processes, or granting any employee the right to stop production to address a quality issue, LEAN accomplishes two all-important goals that are often thought of as competing with one another. LEAN maximizes productivity *and* puts people first.

If you know Donn Sorensen both professionally and personally, you know that he embodies the spirit of LEAN. That two-dimensional commitment to efficiency and employee engagement that is promoted in LEAN is found in Donn and his philosophy and practice of leadership.

I serve with Donn on a variety of boards, not the least of which is the Mercy Health System board, where I serve as the vice chairman of Mercy East as well chairman of the Patient Safety and Quality Committee for the Mercy East Communities. I also serve as a member on the Mercy Ministry Board's Patient Safety and Quality Committee. In those positions, I've observed that Donn has a simple approach to leadership, but one that is very effective. Over the years, he's mastered the art of implementing what the medical management business calls the Integrated Delivery System (IDS) structure, which, among other things, simplifies complicated processes, eliminates waste and needless repetition of work, and above all, increases the involvement and engagement of both physicians and managers. The structure is very effective. Donn has been able to use it with great success; he and his team have improved business in pretty much every key indicator, from gaining significantly in market share to dramatically increasing revenue.

But you won't find any of the details of how the IDS system works in this book. In fact, you won't find any of the details and minutiae that, good or bad, you might find in other books on management and leadership. Complex theories and lengthy philosophies have their place, but that isn't Donn—and that's not what his *Big-Hearted Leadership* is about.

In this book, he's really giving leaders a LEAN-like approach to being someone who balances effectiveness with emotional intelligence. His five basic principles are simple (simple, not easy) and, if modeled correctly, they are profoundly effective. The strength of this book is that it's straightforward and actionable. There are a lot of worthy discussions to have that Donn (wisely) doesn't get into. There are details that, while helpful, might bog you down.

Donn's hope—and I think he's successful—is to give you a book that shows you how to be effective and caring at the same time. I'm happy to call Donn Sorensen a friend and colleague. I'm also happy to recommend this fine book, which shows that you can have the best of both worlds as a leader. You can be a caring, Big-Hearted Leader because it is the right thing to do. And it's good for business.

–George Roman
Principal, Roman Consulting LLC

# Acknowledgments

I'D LIKE TO START BY THANKING MY CHILDREN, Alec and Jenna, for giving me the privilege of being your dad. I love you! To my family: thank you for all that you've done for me. I wouldn't be where or who I am without you.

To my many great friends: there are too many to name; you know who you are. I love you all!

Thanks to Vaughn Kohler, my writing collaborator, who helped me articulate my ideas and put them to paper. You are one talented wordsmith, my friend.

And, of course, I can't help but express my gratitude to God. He has given me far more blessings than I deserve.

# Introduction

---

"YOU CAN'T LEAD THE PEOPLE
IF YOU DON'T LOVE THE PEOPLE."

**CORNEL WEST**

---

---

"PEOPLE DON'T CARE HOW MUCH YOU KNOW
UNTIL THEY KNOW HOW MUCH YOU CARE."

**RICK WARREN**

---

HUMILITY IS A FINE QUALITY IN A LEADER (AND GOOD
for the soul), so let me begin with a somewhat embar-

rassing confession: I love stupid movies.

The more stupid the movie, the more I like it. I mean, I love cornball classics like *Animal House*, *Airplane*, and *Dumb and Dumber*. If I've watched them once, I've watched them a thousand times. I know the scripts front to back and probably even side to side.

One of my favorites is *Tommy Boy*. Chris Farley stars as the hapless and hilarious protagonist, Tommy Callahan. Fresh off a post-secondary education that took almost a decade ("You know, a lot of people go to college for seven years!"), Tommy is the would-be heir of Callahan Auto, but he bungled and botched his first attempts at sales. Eventually, Tommy played to his strengths. In the immortal words of Richard Hayden (played by David Spade), "There are two types of smart: book smart, which waved bye-bye to you a long time ago, and then there's street smart, the ability to read people. And you have that, just like your dad. He was the best at knowing what people wanted to hear and what people needed to hear." In the end, the goofy Tommy proved himself to be an incredible leader. He saved Callahan Auto by closing the deal of a lifetime.

Richard said Tommy had street smarts. I say Tommy was an intelligent, effective leader who had something many don't: a big heart.

Better to have a big heart than a big ego, right? I don't want to go on and on about myself, but the best way for me to explain what I mean is by telling you a little about my life and the successes I've enjoyed in business.

Maybe the reason I've always identified with Tommy Callahan is because book smarts don't come naturally to me, either. While I was the son of a college professor, I struggled with academics. From elementary school to high school, I did well enough on my schoolwork to get by, but not much better than that. In time, I discovered that I had a learning disability, but this revelation didn't make me feel much better about my academic success. I grew up with a subtle tendency toward mediocrity and underachievement.

Thankfully, I was good at sports, and through a track scholarship I was admitted to Luther College in Iowa, a school with high academic standards. The minute I stepped onto campus, I knew that I was in over my head. I didn't know how I was going to run track, study, and enjoy my college years. I had to hit the books hard just to survive. But I did it! In 1980, I graduated with a business degree.

Shortly thereafter, I landed a management trainee job with Mayo Clinic, and at that point I thought I was set. I had a decent-paying job, a girlfriend, an apartment, a car—and no ambition.

Then I had a life-defining moment. Sitting at my workstation at the Mayo Clinic, I overheard two men talking. It wasn't the most profound conversation, but it struck me. One of the guys simply said to the other, "I think you could end up being one of the top managers in the nation."

I heard that, and a question popped into my head:

*Why couldn't I be one of the top-ranked managers in the nation?*

Right there, in a matter-of-fact sort of way, I shed my commitment to underachievement. I asserted the first real, red-blooded ambition of my life (at least the first non-athletic ambition). I said, "That's what I'm going to do. I'm going to become a manager, an executive—a leader—who is nationally known." Changing my intention made all the difference in the world. Because I reset the expectations I held for myself, I was able to achieve much more than I once thought possible.

> Right there, in a matter-of-fact sort of way, I shed my commitment to underachievement.

Over the past few decades, I've earned my spurs and accolades in the medical practice management business and worked with the best and brightest physicians and leaders in the healthcare field. Most significantly, I've served as chief operating officer of Mercy Health in Springfield, Missouri and currently serve as the president of Mercy East Region in St. Louis.

My team and I have been able to accomplish some amazing things in the Mercy Health System. Today, the Mercy Health System is very successful. We enjoy the goodwill of the community, we excel in market share, and we're consistently identified as one of the top healthcare systems in the nation. But most importantly, we deliver quality care with a commitment to compassion—and that combination of effectiveness and empathy is what I champion most of all. It is what directs everything I do as I seek to lead the organization I serve.

From time to time, especially at watershed moments, I've been asked to articulate my philosophy or approach to leadership. When I reflect on a career that now spans more than thirty years, I tell people that I haven't built my best management teams with brainiacs from Ivy League schools. I have nothing against Ivy Leaguers—not at all. But what I really want—and what has translated into success time and time again—are qualified people who have big hearts. My philosophy is this: have a big heart and lead with it.

This is a book about being an effective and intelligent leader with a big heart. It's a book about taking the company or organization you serve and the people on your team to greater heights of success through what I call "Big-Hearted Leadership." Now, at this point, I don't blame you if you have some questions:

1. What does a big heart have to do with good business?

2. Does compassion really figure into my competency as a leader?

By the time you finish reading this book, I hope you'll see that the answers to your questions are:

1. A lot.

2. Absolutely.

In the meantime, though, know that I'm in good company when I say that having a big heart is good for business. Chade-Meng Tan is a software engineer and motivational speaker who calls himself "the Jolly Good Fellow" of Google. Over the last couple years, he has served that giant company as head of personal growth.

He is part of a team for the nonprofit organization One Billion Acts of Peace, which was nominated for the 2015 Nobel Peace Prize. He developed a training course, which later became a book called *Search Inside Yourself.* In that book, he cites the opinions of Bill George, the well-respected former CEO of Medtronic, as well as the findings of Gary Collins, author of the mega-bestselling book *Good to Great.* And he arrives at an undeniable conclusion: *compassion is a common quality of the most effective leaders.*

Those guys did their homework. In this book, I do not claim to have exhaustively studied the issue from an academic perspective. I have never personally performed any detailed, formal research on the relationship between compassion and effective leadership. But I will tell you this: the conclusions of Tan, George, Collins, and many others like them are 100 percent confirmed by my own experience as a leader.

Let's take just one issue I have experienced in my career in medical practice management: the physician/patient relationship. At Mercy, our physicians share leadership at every level of the organization. Whether they are presenting to our board or diagnosing a patient, we want them to be the most effective leaders they can be. So what does that look like? Well, consider this:

Do people want a first-rate physician? Of course. They deserve one! Does it matter if that doctor is a jerk or not? It sure does. In fact, it matters so much you can put a price tag on it.

From time to time, we all hear about a lawsuit involving medical malpractice. A doctor makes a mistake because, well, they aren't perfect. They are human beings like everyone else. Sometimes the mistake is significant and results in real difficulty for the patient. In those situations, you might think that the error always results in a lawsuit. Well, if you think that, you'd be wrong. The reality is that there is a certain kind of doctor who almost never gets sued. Decades-old studies have shown that doctors who take the time to gently educate their patients, laugh and cry with them, listen to them, and give them the opportunity to express their own thoughts and feelings hardly ever face legal action. Simply put, people generally don't sue physicians who *care*. As a result, health systems save millions in legal fees and malpractice payouts. That's just one example of how compassion—or a lack thereof—can affect the bottom line.

So, yes, big hearts and good business do go together. Compassion does figure into your competency as a leader.

If I were one of those aforementioned Ivy Leaguers, I might start by offering a really clear, comprehensive definition of Big-Hearted Leadership. But I'm a simple, practical guy (abstraction waved bye-bye to me a long time ago). Instead, in the chapters that follow, I'll share straightforward principles and concrete practices that will help you see what Big-Hearted Leadership looks like. Seeing what a Big-Hearted Leader does will help you understand what Big-Hearted Leadership is.

> Compassion—or a lack thereof—can affect the bottom line.

First, though, let's clear up any negative assumptions and potential misunderstandings by talking about what Big-Hearted Leadership is not.

## Big-Hearted Leadership is not about syrup and sentimentalism, but intelligence and action.

For good reason, the heart is associated with emotion. But it would be missing the point to conclude that Big-Hearted Leadership is about sentiment. Sure, as you'll discover, a good leader should be sensitive, compassionate, and caring. A leader should do his or her best to develop what experts call "emotional intelligence," but I'm not in the business of encouraging leaders to be spineless saps. Effective leaders have minds and they are called to use them. They have wills and they are called to assert them to make tough decisions. So if you hear "heart" and you think "syrup" and "sentimentalism," you're wrong. Big-Hearted Leadership isn't about weakness. It's about strength, and you must practice in order to get strong. Remember: the heart is a muscle.

## Big-Hearted Leadership is not about "Rah! Rah!" and relationships *at the expense* of sound policies, protocols, and structure.

I'm a relationship guy. I love people. I am absolutely energized by interacting with my team or going out and socializing with friends. I love motivating people, leading the charge, and doing what I can to rally the troops. I put a high premium on vibrant *esprit de corps.* But I've learned that the interpersonal only thrives within a good infrastructure—we'll talk about that in chapter one.

You can deliver inspirational speeches and give one-on-one pep talks all you want, but the talk has to find a way to walk. Administration is necessary and essential. Structure as well as sound policies and protocols are a must.

## Big-Hearted Leadership is not warm fuzzies *at the expense of* cold, hard cash.

I may sound too much like Pollyanna, but I don't have many bad days at my job. Occasionally they happen, but I don't make it a point to remember them. Most of the time I have good days—even great days. I love my job and that's because it's not just a job. It's a calling. It's part of who I am. I'm passionate about the mission of Mercy Health and from time to time, I get emotional thinking about all the great work done by our physicians and staff and the lives they impact on a daily basis.

> Without revenue, the cause dies.

But you know what? What we do at the ministry of Mercy Health still has a strong business component, and a main goal of a business—any business—is to make money. Without funds, you can't pay employees. Without capital, you can't build bigger and better resources. Without revenue, the cause dies.

Some may consider it inconsistent to think a

leader in a mission-driven nonprofit organization would consider making money important. But those people would be wrong. We owe it to those who rely on our services to keep our businesses—mine and yours— strong and vibrant.

Bottom line: you won't get warm fuzzies without cold hard cash, because you won't have the resources to do the things that bring the warm fuzzies. So if you think Big-Hearted Leadership isn't concerned about revenue, you're crazy.

## Big Hearted Leadership is not about being religious or spiritual, but about being good and decent.

I feel like I need to make this clear. Just because I serve an organization that was founded by the Sisters of Mercy and has a strong spiritual component does not mean that my message is limited to leaders of religiously affiliated organizations. Hardly! I might quote the Good Book here and there, but I'm using it to illustrate rather than to evangelize. Truth is truth, whether it comes from the mouth of St. Stephen or Steve Jobs. Leaders can be kind and compassionate, whether they are agnostic or ardent in their spiritual faith. The spiritual references I've incorporated into this book are included because they are part of who I am and the milieu in which I work. But you can express Big-Hearted Leadership through your own creeds or convictions. You can apply the principles in any organization, sacred or secular.

\* \* \*

Now I'd like to tell you how to read this book: any way you want to. Sure, I think it's a good idea to read chapter one first, but after that you can skip around depending on what topics catch your attention and are most relevant to your situation and needs. There's no one-size-fits-all leader. Let your heart be your guide.

# CHAPTER ONE:
## Give Your People a Structure They Can Lean On

---

*"Good order is the foundation of all things."*

EDMUND BURKE

---

WHEN I WAS RUNNING TRACK IN HIGH SCHOOL AND college, I was in the best shape of my life. I invested hours and hours of training and ran miles and miles. I was lean and limber. Heck, my body fat percentage was probably a negative number.

While all that effort won me races and medals, it was obviously good for my cardiovascular health, too. I could do a quick sprint and only breathe a little harder. My resting pulse rate was about forty beats a minute.

No doubt about it: I had a very, very strong heart.

Strong hearts aren't just necessary for athletes. They're essential for everyone. Without a heart, you have no life.

Yes, I know that's obvious. But . . .

A heart without a ribcage to protect it would be dangerously vulnerable. A heart and vascular system without a skeletal system to prop it up would collapse into a bloody, unsightly mess.

The same holds true in business. People are at the very heart of a company, relationships are the lifeblood of an organization—we hear that all the time. But without a good structure to support them, things are going to get messy—really messy.

So, before they do anything else, Big-Hearted Leaders must provide a sound organizational structure that supports their people. And here's a point I can't make strongly enough: this isn't just a good business practice, it's the very first way that you show the people in your business or organization that you care about them. The quality of people's work experience—which will influence the quality of their lives—is directly tied to the quality of the structure their leader provides.

Don't buy that? Well, consider the hell that leaders

put people through when there is either bad structure or no structure at all.

## Overly Complicated Decision-Making Process

You ever heard of Rube Goldberg? He was an American cartoonist, sculptor, engineer, and inventor. He's best known for drawing complicated gadgets that perform simple tasks in indirect, convoluted ways. Go to YouTube, type in "Rube Goldberg machines," and you can watch complex contraptions do things like push a doorbell or crack an egg.

A bad structure or no structure at all can make the decision-making process resemble a Rube Goldberg invention. It becomes far more complicated than it needs to be. Think about how many decisions are made every day in a small- to mid-sized business. Now think about how many more decisions are made in a large organization. Every decision brings with it certain results and ramifications. If the structure isn't solid, the decision-making process becomes more whimsical, idiosyncratic, and arbitrary—and the potential for chaos and conflict skyrockets.

## No Safety Net nor Backup Plan

Without structure, a leader is not providing a safety net or backup plan for dealing with crises. Regardless of an organization's size, unexpected things happen. For years, children, emergency-services personnel, and industrial workers have been taught a simple phrase: stop, drop, and roll! I'm sure it's difficult to focus when you're on fire, but think of how many people have stayed calm and saved themselves by following this straightforward fire-safety technique.

It's no different in business; when things catch fire, people need to stay calm and default to basic principles, processes, and protocols established by a good structure. If those things don't exist, people panic.

## A Lack of Shared Goals

If a leader doesn't provide structure, the goals of the team will not be aligned. When a team is pursuing separate goals, one goal ends up being counterproductive to achieving another. For example, one department of a company could find itself in competition with another. Without a clear direction and set goals, your people have no idea which way the company is headed.

This causes confusion and apprehension and, ultimately, there will be no alignment with customers either. How can a company without clear goals and direction create a product or deliver a service that will satisfy? It can't.

All of these factors lead to situations that are massively unfair to the people in an organization. The lack of a good structure exacerbates interpersonal conflict and all but ensures the failure of the organization. When a good structure is not in place, you end up with lousy communication between individuals and departments and things don't work the way they should. For instance, in the medical management industry, it is not at all uncommon for a faulty structure to lead to separate groups within that system duplicating tasks. (This can happen in any field or industry.) Worse yet, a bad structure can actually result in individual departments competing against each other. A hospital and clinic in the same healthcare system might both come up with a new service to offer patients. But instead of uniting their efforts, avoiding duplicate work, and sharing resources, they find themselves at cross-purposes. Ultimately, all of this happens because the structure lacks integration. No one has looked at it carefully to determine whether it provides for distinctions between activities that can and should be conducted by single departments and those that are best accomplished by cooperative effort. In addition, there are usually no policies and protocols in place that let people know what assets and resources the organization possesses and what can be shared.

Remember what Abraham Lincoln said about "a house divided"? Whether it's a hospital system, a nutritional supplement company, or a retail chain, a business without a good structure cannot stand.

In the end, people often feel devalued in an organization without a sound structure. Dissatisfaction skyrockets. Morale plummets. The blame game starts. Relationships suffer. The business fails. In the words of Tommy Callahan's buddy Richard Hayden in *Tommy Boy*, "You have derailed."

Big-Hearted Leaders don't take good, hard-working people and put them in a situation ripe for conflict and rigged for failure.

## Finding a Good Structure

Big-Hearted Leaders make structure the first priority. If you care about your people and if you care about success, creating a good structure is the first thing you'll do.

A good structure is one that codifies and simplifies the decision-making process; provides a safety net or backup plan for crises; and provides alignment for goals, management, and direction.

Again, those are general guidelines. It's up to you to find the structure that works well for your business or organization. Since each situation is different, I can't tell you what structure is going to work for you in detail, but here are five things that can help you:

> Spoiler alert: if you're losing revenue or your gains are decreasing, you've got a bad structure.

## 1. Consider the obvious.

There's a good chance you have a good structure if you can answer yes to the following three questions:

**Are we making money?** Spoiler alert: if you're losing revenue or your gains are decreasing, you've got a bad structure. And there's no better indicator of a good structure than not only creating revenue but increasing it.

**Are employees happy?** Repeat after me: structure affects the interpersonal. If your business or organization has all the right policies, protocols, and procedures, it should directly and positively affect the mental and emotional health of your people. Structure leads to smiles. Yes, every company has complainers and malcontents, but when things work well because a solid structure is supporting the organization, the vast majority of people are satisfied, energized, and happy.

**Does the nearby community embrace you?** There's nothing better than walking into a restaurant or church and having someone come up to you and say, "Man, you guys over there at [insert company] really have it together. Your [product or service] was so helpful to me and my family. We love you guys!" If this happens to you a lot, it is a sign you have a good structure.

## 2. Draw from your experience.

When I joined the effort to help transform Mercy Health in Springfield, Missouri, and later Mercy East Region in St. Louis, I knew exactly what structure was needed. I had already used the Integrated Delivery System with great success over the last thirty years of my career. If you've been in business for any length of time, you can draw from your experience, too. It may well be the case that you have used a structure that works, but, for whatever reason, forgot about it or deviated from it. Experience is a great teacher, but sometimes to tap into its wisdom you need to actively think about what you've done in the past. Sit down and think through your history in business. What were your most successful ventures? When were you the most productive? Think about the structure and organization of your business at that time and consider whether it is something you can recreate now.

## 3. Always lean toward LEAN.

My friend George Roman served as a top executive for the Boeing Company for more than thirty-three years. Today, he's a business consultant. He helps clients all over the world succeed by implementing disciplined and measurable processes to help them accomplish their goals in a far more efficient way. Later in his career, he learned of a systematic manufacturing method originally implemented by the Toyota Motor Company in Japan but innovated and applied brilliantly by Boeing. That method is often referred to as "LEAN" manufacturing or the "LEAN" method.

I love LEAN. I've had the opportunity to walk through the Boeing factories myself here in St. Louis and observe LEAN in real life. I marveled as fighter jet after fighter jet rolled off of their line. I've also implemented LEAN principles and processes at the company I serve.

I love LEAN because it promotes the best of both worlds. It is remarkable at eliminating waste, making the complicated simple, and keeping only those actions or processes that truly add value. But it doesn't achieve those goals at the expense of people. Quite the opposite: the LEAN process values employees and increases their involvement. For instance, two core principles of LEAN are (1) the continual educational development of employees and (2) granting employees on every level the authority to halt production if they identify a threat to quality. Suffice it to say, LEAN is not an either/or kind of system. It is a both/and.

Obviously, this is not the place to go into a point-by-point explanation of LEAN. My point is that there is already a tried and true organizational method in existence that values and promotes both productivity and people. In my opinion, the LEAN structure and a Big-Hearted leader are a match made in heaven!

And just in case you're wondering: if your business doesn't involve manufacturing, that's okay. The basic principles and processes of LEAN can be almost universally applied. (By the way, books on LEAN are legion.

But you can check out *The Toyota Way* by Jeffrey K. Liker for a good overview and explanation.)

The bottom line is that the structure you choose should operate on the same principles as LEAN. Does your structure have all the fat trimmed off it? Does it place equal value on productivity and people? If it's not LEAN, it better be like it.

## 4. Make it good, not perfect.

I once heard former United States Secretary of State Condoleezza Rice say, "Don't let the perfect be the enemy of the good." Turns out she might've gotten that little maxim from the French writer and philosopher Voltaire. Either way, it's true. Finding a good structure for your business or organization isn't the same as finding a perfect structure. You'll never do that. In the same way, don't start worrying that you've got a bad structure simply because you encounter some challenges right out of the gate. Don't second-guess yourself because the early stages of implementation are full of chaos and craziness. Trust me: the chaos will settle. The craziness will subside. Press on. You'll never have that close-to-perfect structure without first having a good-enough structure you can improve upon.

## 5. Once You Settle, Start Selling

Once you've evaluated your options and settled on a good structure, start selling it. If you lead a major organization, start by promoting your structure to the board of directors and upper-level management. And do it with *passion*! Think of yourself and your board like evangelists. You've been given a structure that is a gift from heaven! Now, you're all on a mission from God to make sure everybody knows about it and how great it is.

Regardless of the size of your business or organization, you should sell your structure to all employees on all levels. Some of this will happen one-on-one or in small groups; some of it (especially for a big business) will happen in larger settings through formal speeches and presentations. If you're really committed, some of it will even happen over lunch or during a friendly tennis match. Sell always and everywhere.

At this point, you might be tempted to follow that old saying, "Under promise and over deliver." Well-known business book author Tom Peters came up with that concept, and he's a smart guy who has built a very successful career. So I don't disagree with him lightly— but I do disagree (sort of). If I understand him correctly, he simply meant that we should exceed expectations.

And that's exactly right. But I also think it's important *to set expectations high from the get-go*. Why?

My experience is consistent: people want to get excited. They want to get behind something big, be a part of something special. So it's your responsibility as the leader to be confident and enthusiastic about the structure you're going to provide and to do everything in your power to spread that confidence and enthusiasm to everyone else. Again: don't under-promise and over-deliver. Promise, promise, promise, and then deliver on your promises.

I'll talk more about the Big-Hearted Leader's responsibility and privilege to constantly sell in another chapter. As you'll discover, I don't really call it "selling" at all. I call it possessing and passing on enduring enthusiasm.

## Implementation: Right Now and with the Right Ratio

### Implement Right Now

Once you find a good structure and start selling it, then what? Implement it, of course. If you have your finger on the pulse of the business and leadership culture right now, you'll read and hear a lot about "change management." There is no shortage of seminars and conferences about the nuts and bolts of transforming your organization according to a particular schedule. "Timing is vital," many management gurus say. "People naturally resist change, so proceed carefully, step gingerly."

Now, there is certainly a lot of wisdom in recognizing that *when* you do something is often as important as *what* you do and *why* you do it. But, speaking from personal experience, the best policy is to move ahead swiftly, smartly, and without fear.

I love the movie *Master and Commander: The Far Side of the World*. In my opinion, it is one of the best naval movies of all time. It's also a great study in leadership. In several scenes, Captain Jack Aubrey (played by Russell Crowe) says, "Quick's the word and sharp's the action!" This is a command that means "Act now!" and "Don't waste time!" For the captain of a huge English warship, this was an important command. A boat that size didn't just turn on a dime. It took time to change course.

Get the analogy? The fact is, your business can sink quickly, but getting it moving in the right direction—or up to speed for the very first time—takes much longer. If you're confident that you've found a good structure, why would you move ahead at a snail's pace? Implement—and implement now. *Quick's the word and sharp's the action!*

## Implement the Right Ratio

You've probably heard of the 80/20 rule in sales or marketing—the Pareto Principle—that 80 percent of your sales come from 20 percent of your clients. Well, this is a different 80/20 rule: 80 percent of the structure is set and 20 percent is flexible. In other words, once you've chosen your structure, the vast majority of it is not up for discussion. You're the leader. You've chosen the structure moving forward and, come hell or high water, there's no give and take. It's set in stone. So you're going to implement that 80 percent—and you're going to do it now, capiche?

The other 20 percent? That's more open for negotiation. When you direct change in an organization where things have been done differently for a long time, there's bound to be histrionics. There will also be factors you don't know about. The milieu and context of your business and the unique idiosyncrasies of your field or industry may call for some tweaking of your structure. Above all, this 20 percent flexibility gives people an opportunity to provide feedback and share leadership. And, unlike the 80 percent, you don't have to hammer out the details of the other 20 percent right away. You can take your time—sometimes years.

## Giving the Heart a Ribcage

I'm privileged to be friends with Isaac Bruce, the outstanding wide receiver who played a critical role in the St. Louis Rams' 1999 championship season. (By the time this book is published, he may be in the Hall of Fame!) I've talked to Isaac a number of times about the years leading up to his Super Bowl appearances in 1999 and 2001. The Rams had been mired in mediocrity. Well, that's being kind. They'd had back-to-back losing seasons for the past four years. Yet it wasn't because the team lacked a strong work ethic. It wasn't because they didn't have talent in key positions. In my opinion, they needed a framework to play better football.

When coach Dick Vermeil and offensive coordinator Mike Martz arrived, they provided a structure that their players could lean on. They installed an offensive system that took already talented and hard-working players and set them up for success. The potential of each member of the team was maximized, and, before you knew it, the sports world marveled at "The Greatest Show on Turf." Throughout the season, that 1999 team shattered every conceivable offensive record, and, as Joe Buck triumphantly shouted at the end of the Super Bowl game, "The gateway to the west . . . [had] become . . . the gateway to the best football team in the land!"

No doubt about it: Isaac Bruce, Kurt Warner, Marshall Faulk, and others were the heart of the team, but Vermeil and Martz gave the heart a ribcage. Big-Hearted Leaders that they were, they provided a structure their players could lean on. The result: Super Bowl champions.

Big-Hearted Leaders care about their people, so the very first thing they do is provide the framework to flourish. It's the right thing to do—and it's good for business.

# CHAPTER TWO:
## Be "Here" and "With"

---

*"Few delights can equal the presence of one
whom we trust utterly."*

GEORGE MACDONALD

---

HAVE YOU EVER SEEN THE MOVIE *We Are Marshall*?
It's a great film about a terrible tragedy, a 1970 plane
crash that resulted in the death of almost every member
of the Marshall University Thundering Herd football
program.

Initially, the school planned to discontinue the football program, but at the urging of the student body they
decided to start the program over again. The university
president, Donald Dedmon, hired coach Jack Lengyel

to help save the Herd from extinction.

In the movie, as Jack starts rebuilding the team, he realizes that there's only one way the program is going to be remotely competitive: if he recruits amazing high-school athletes by telling them that they can play right away. Just one problem: at the time the NCAA didn't allow freshmen to play. Lengyel asks Dedmon to convince the NCAA to make an exception to its policy. Dedmon dutifully calls the NCAA and dashes off letter after letter—to no avail. His request is denied again and again.

Demoralized, Dedmon shows up at practice to lament his failure. Not deterred at all, Jack Lengyel motivates the university president with a pep talk.

*Jack: Let me ask you a question. Now, are you married?*

*Don: Yes, I am. Twenty-five years in May.*

*Jack: Twenty-five years . . . I am willing to bet you didn't propose over the phone.*

*Don: No, I didn't.*

*Jack: Okay. And I know damn well that she didn't say yes in a letter.*

*Don: Jack?*

*Jack: Doc?*

*Don: No, Jack. I know.*

*Jack: Yes, Doc. You can do it. You're an outlaw. Pioneer. Gunslinger. This is a whole new game, Doc.*

In the scenes that follow, the university president goes to Kansas City and pleads his case, ultimately winning the support of the NCAA. Donald Dedmon, Coach Jack Lengyel, and Marshall University won their appeal through the power of presence. Big-Hearted Leaders succeed through the same power of personal attention to people.

## Our Disembodied Digital Age

Our digital age is a largely disembodied age. Whether we are browsing the Internet, sending or receiving an email, or texting and talking on our phones, our attention is directed toward affairs that are taking place away from us. A significant amount of our work involves people who are not in our physical presence. In spite of this, human nature doesn't change. We aren't going to lose our desire or need to be with other people.

Brian Solis, a digital analyst, anthropologist, and futurist says, "Telepresence can never make up for the heart-to-heart connection two people experience when they are in the same room." Similarly, Arianna Huffington, the media mogul who has made millions through the Huffington Post and other online platforms, has frequently argued in her books and speeches that as the use of technology increases, people will not want less human touch. They will want more.

**A Big-Hearted Leader makes it his or her priority to be present and accessible . . .**

Big-Hearted Leaders happily give their people what they want and need. A Big-Hearted Leader makes it his or her priority to be present and accessible, to be here and with, regardless of the size of the organization. Now, obviously, if your organization has thousands of employees, you can't be literally present for all of them. But you darn sure better make yourself present and accessible to the core leadership, influencers, and stakeholders. Model your ideal presence and accessibility, and there should be a trickle-down effect.

Here are four strategies for you to adopt and practice:

# 1. Opt for in-person over electronic forms of communication.

Eschew electronic communication and remember that everybody needs your body. By now, you've probably read in a lot of the popular business literature that there are some serious drawbacks to email and other forms of electronic communication like texting or even phone calls.

As I see it, this is the problem: emails are text-based and text has its limitations. When you send emails, the text can't reflect the subtle nuances in your tone of voice. It can't communicate your facial expressions. Even if you go the route of Skype or webinars, there's still something missing. The image of a person is not a person. The sound of a human voice is different when it is transferred through a microphone and speaker.

Ultimately, the problem is that when you use electronic platforms, people are getting their leader second-hand. They are communicating with a facsimile of you—not you.

If you don't think this is a big deal, ask yourself a couple of questions: Why do so many military marriages break up after the soldier is deployed for a year or longer? Well, obviously there might be multiple issues at play. But one extremely relevant factor is that it's hard to sustain a relationship when you aren't physically present to one another. Why don't the delegates to the United Nations just log in and conduct their business and diplomacy through the web? Because the whole history of human relations has proven that when the stakes are high, you have to show up in person. You have to be there.

Why do you suppose in-person communication is so necessary to a relationship's success? I'm sure philosophers and sociologists and other academics have their well-thought-out theories. But as near as I can tell, the reason is this: communication is about 90 percent body language. There's an almost magical transference that takes place when people are in one another's presence. Take away the body and you just denied yourself that opportunity for transference and reduced your communication efficiency to 10 percent.

## There's Power in Your Posture

Stand in a room with another person. Head up, shoulders back, chest out—you can project both calm and confidence. That's when mirror neurons do their work. Ever heard of those things? According to the American Psychological Association, a mirror neuron "fires when an animal acts and when the animal observes the same action performed by another. Thus, the neuron 'mirrors' the behavior of the other, as if the observer were itself acting." The same thing happens in humans; in layman's terms, it means people unconsciously mimic what they see in others. So you can inspire with your posture. Person-to-person, confidence is contagious. Stand tall, Big-Hearted Leader—and there's a better chance your team will, too!

## There's Something Engaging about Eye Contact

When was the last time you felt you really engaged with someone staring at you through a computer screen? Not recently, I'm sure. When you stand in a room and lock eyes with someone, you immediately show that person that he or she has your full attention. When I say "lock eyes," I don't mean zero in on them with eyes like Hannibal Lecter; I mean focus. Don't let your eyes constantly dart from one end of the room to the other. At that moment, look at that other person like he or she is the most important person in the world. Do you think giving your full attention makes someone feel valued? Absolutely. Does it motivate people in a way electronic communication can't? Yes, it does.

## There's Something Spellbinding about a Smile

Can you smile at someone through email? Well, you can use an emoticon—let me know how that works for you. You can "smile when you dial," and at least some of the warmth will be transferred through the phone line. And yes, people can see you smile on a computer screen. But answer me this: would you rather listen to an album of your favorite band or go to a live concert? One is just listening; the other is an experience. It's the same when you show your pearly whites in person. Your people won't just see you smile—they will experience it. And the connection that forms through that experience will be priceless. There's certainly a mountain of scientific evidence that shows smiling has incredibly positive interpersonal effects. I won't cite any studies because, frankly, I think that's common sense. I'll just wrap up this section with a quote from a little woman whose life impacted millions. Mother Teresa said, "We shall never know all the good that a simple smile can do."

## There's Something Persuasive about Personal Touch

A handshake. A pat on the back. Even a fist bump. These can do something that electronic communication can't—they establish emotional connection in a powerful way. You're not just wishing your people well; you're demonstrating your well wishes with your actions. You aren't just saying you care; you're showing it.

Of course, it should go without saying that you have to exercise discretion. Part of being a good leader is knowing what the members of your team are comfortable with—and what they are not. Giving a trusted advisor a warm pat on the back is safe. Giving a hug to an employee you barely know? Not such a great idea—regardless of your good intentions. When in doubt, ask your HR directors. They are there to help you preserve the integrity of office relationships.

> Instead of psychological pressure, your personal touch can promote psychological well-being.

Still, I can't stress enough how positively powerful personal touch can be. Back in the day, sales people used to be coached to put their hand on someone's shoulder when they asked, "Are you ready to purchase this fine vehicle?" They knew it added psychological pressure. Well, that's manipulation, but it's also sound science. And what they used to meet a sales quota can be used for good. Instead of psychological pressure, your personal touch can promote psychological well-being. You can positively influence through personal touch. In fact, Dr. Dacher Keltner, a psychology professor at the University of California–Berkeley, said, "A pat on the back, a caress on the arm—these are incidental gestures we usually take for granted, but . . . they are far more profound than we realize. [Touch is] a language that is essential to being human." Michelangelo, one of the greatest geniuses of all time, said, "To touch is to give life."

## 2. Go out and about for coffee and lunch breaks.

I know it seems inefficient to leave your office in order to connect with people, but sometimes things that are more effective take more time. When you have a break in your day, whether it is for lunch or coffee, intentionally go down the hall, maybe onto another floor, and get your coffee. This will give you the opportunity to pass people in the halls, to engage them casually, and put your presence in their minds. It will give you the opportunity to get near them, to be where they are, introduce yourself into their environment, and, by doing so, make yourself more accessible and approachable.

The other benefit to going out and about is it gets you moving. Saint Augustine, the great philosopher and theologian, once said, "*Solvitur ambulando,*" which is

Latin for "It is solved by walking." There's something about movement that can churn up your thoughts in a good way, getting your creative juices and logic going. This is supported by science—look it up. Movement is good.

Plus, it's a good way to get the pulse and find out what's going on. You'll pick up the scuttlebutt, the inside scoop, and you may learn things in those informal settings that you wouldn't in a formal meeting. But above all, you'll be visible, smiling, and warm, and that's enough to make the walk worth it.

## 3. Schedule regular lunches, feedback sessions, and meetings.

In addition to being present and accessible in informal ways, you'll want to schedule regular times to have lunch with various personnel in the company. If yours is a large corporation, schedule times to have lunch with different departments. Meet with more than one person but not a huge group; five is a good number. And remember to be mindful to the importance of your eating environment. Sure, you can have a great meeting at a corporate cafeteria or chain restaurant, but why not dine at a place that's special to you? My favorite place to grab a bite here in the St. Louis area is Café Napoli in Clayton. The food is great, the ambiance is terrific, the service is friendly and professional, and Han Tran the bartender is a magician when it comes to cocktails. Most importantly, they know me and I know them. So when I go there, it's more than eating out on the town; it's a meal among friends. I believe that personal connection and sense of familiarity with the restaurant and its staff will be transferred to your party. The intimacy of the experience will be enhanced.

When you are having lunch, just let there be small talk. Listen a lot. If you have a group of complainers, just listen and smile and take it. You'll know when it's important and you have to take action or offer an explanation. You're there to listen, engage, and be present to your team. If you are in a big group, don't get into debates with people—you never end up looking good, even if you are right, and by engaging in a battle you will encourage others to argue with you. The sharks will smell blood and will come out to fight. Bottom line: just listen and take mental notes. If something is legitimate, think about it—and act on it. In some cases, you may want to follow up with the person whose feedback you responded to. It's good to let people know the changes they suggested were actually made.

## 4. Enlist others to go with you.

There will be times when being present means enlisting coworkers to come with you to certain events. People kid with me that I often bring my "Donntourage" with me. That doesn't bother me; I'm happy to build friendships. Of course, you risk the possibility that some people are going to accuse you of having favorites. So be it. Leaders are human beings, too; they should be allowed to have some people they connect with and get along with more than others.

## For Those Who Object

I realize that some of you reading this right now may struggle with the concept of making yourself physically present and accessible on a regular basis. It's not that you don't see some logic in it. But you're resisting because one of three objections just came to your mind.

**"I'm not a people person."** I know, I know. You agree with Linus from the *Peanuts* comic strip when he said, "I love humanity. It's people I can't stand!" If given the chance, you'd rather brainstorm on a whiteboard than pick the brain of a board member. Ten times out of ten, you'll prefer sitting behind your desk to standing behind a podium. Office socials and holiday parties? They're not for you.

In my opinion, you have two options. First, you can develop a strong relationship with a colleague also in a leadership position who is willing to offer physical presence on your behalf in some cases. This is not without precedent. The late, great Steve Jobs and his Apple colleague Paul Allen made a great team. Allen was mostly a behind-the-scenes guy; Jobs was the front man. They were very different in how they operated; yet together, they were supremely effective. You could set up the same type of situation with another leader on your staff.

Or there's the second option: you can just admit that you're really not a leader after all. Does that hurt? I confess: I meant it to sting.

All considerations of technology aside, businesses don't run on automation. They run on people. To be a leader who says, "I'm not a people person," is like being a basketball player who says, "I don't dribble." Become a people person—or get out of the game.

**"I'm not charismatic or outgoing."** Now, this is similar to the first objection, except that it is understandable. A lot of leaders—even lower-level executives—are not what I call "operators." They aren't charismatic, life-of-the-party types. If anything, they would classify themselves as introverts. You know what? That's no problem at all. I'm not asking you to be outgoing. I'm asking you to *go out*. You don't have to be loud and talkative. You don't have to crack jokes (although I suspect you have more of a sense of humor than you think). You just have to be *there*. Stand with fellow workers at the coffeemaker. Look them in the eye. Smile. Pat them on the back. Listen. You can stay your meek, quiet, and gentle self and still be a powerful presence in the lives of your employees.

**"I'm just flat-out scared."** I've been around businesspeople and executives long enough to know that being a president or CEO does not make you immune to fear. Some of the most accomplished leaders I know have, at times, struggled with being self-conscious and insecure. Everybody is human. To a greater or lesser extent, we all care what other people think. We want them to like us.

All I can say is this: The best way to gain confidence to step out and engage other people is to 1) put the focus on them, and 2) think of the conversation as an act of service. In other words, take your ego out of the equation. Now, there's certainly no shortage of ego in my own personality, so if I can do it, so can you. The first line in Rick Warren's massively popular book, *The Purpose-Driven Life*, is this: "It's not about you." Before you talk to anyone, repeat this to yourself again and again: *It's not about me.*

That leads into my second point: don't use the conversation as an opportunity to impress people. Don't think of it as a chance to put your knowledge, wit, and wisdom on display. Instead, ask yourself: How can this conversation help the person I'm talking to? How can it serve their needs? Mostly, you'll help just by listening. Occasionally, though, you'll have the opportunity to better their day by sharing some advice or a word of encouragement—just be sure you're sharing this advice for their benefit, not yours.

## Here and With Is the Way to Win

In some ways, being a leader is like being a successful professional athlete. There's a level of separation between you and your team that isn't completely unlike the level of separation between a player and the fans. That space can lead to you being misunderstood and misinterpreted.

My buddy Jim Edmonds is a seven-time Gold

Glove Award–winning center fielder, a World Series champion (2006), and a St. Louis Cardinals Hall of Famer. Throughout his career, he combined natural speed and athleticism with an uncanny instinct for anticipating where the baseball was going before it was hit. Ask any Redbirds fan and they'll gush about the plays that guy used to make—especially his walk-off, game-winning home run in the 2004 National League Championship Series.

Given his talent, accolades, and—oh, by the way— his model good looks, you might conclude that he's too successful to be a nice guy. Throw into the mix the fact that Jim is pretty laid back and you might misinterpret him as aloof and standoffish. No doubt there's some fan out there who thinks Jim Edmonds is full of himself. That fan would be dead wrong. Get to know him and you'll discover that underneath the calm, cool demeanor is a heart of compassion and a willingness to use his fame to help others. (He's contributed to more charity events than I can think of right now.) Start up a conversation with him and you'll find that sports stereotypes

> Nothing is more effective in overcoming the separation that stifles success than being "here and with."

don't apply: he's a humble, thoughtful man. Be *with* him—and you'll be even more impressed *by* him.

Leaders don't want to be misunderstood or misinterpreted. They want to enjoy the strong relationships that are essential to good business. Nothing is more effective in overcoming the separation that stifles success than being "here and with." So get in the game and be present to the people you serve. As the legendary St. Louis Cardinal broadcaster Jack Buck used to say, "That's a winner!"

# CHAPTER THREE:
## Be Generous in Your Genuineness

---

*"Find out who you are and do it on purpose."*
**DOLLY PARTON**

---

THROUGHOUT HISTORY, LEADERS IN ANY INDUSTRY or area of life have been scrutinized constantly. Yet especially in this social media–driven day and age when people can easily share their opinions with large audiences who can then spread those same opinions to their own spheres of influence, the scrutiny can be both intense and widespread. It may not be just one person who asks, "Why can't you be more like Steve Jobs? Seth Godin? Warren Buffet?" It may be hundreds of thousands of people demanding that you be other than who you are. Many leaders surrender to the pressure—and become who they think people want them to be.

Big-Hearted Leaders reject that way of thinking. They realize that the best thing they can do for their people is to be themselves. Of course, I'm talking about being real. Offer up who you are—nothing more or less. Give people the authentic you—freely and liberally. Or, as I like to say, *be generous in your genuineness*. In my way of thinking, this involves two things: transparency about faults and failures (yours and others') and exercising the freedom to show genuine and heartfelt affection.

> Offer up who you are—nothing more or less.

## Value Vulnerability

Instead of being the kind of leader who makes him or herself unapproachable or unassailable, you should be the first person to say when you've screwed up. In other words, give them your weaknesses, not just your strengths.

If you screw up, don't justify it or rationalize it or even ignore it. Admit it. This takes humility and that alone makes it a daunting prospect, but the really scary part is that admitting your faults is like opening up your chest and setting your heart and your ego side-by-side on the boardroom table. Sitting there all opened up and vulnerable, anybody could start hacking away at them with a machete. The good news is that vulnerability is an outstanding quality in a leader—and an effective one.

Back in 2010, scholar Brené Brown delivered a TED Talk that became wildly popular. It was called "The Power of Vulnerability." In her book *Daring Greatly*, she further unpacked some of the ideas in her talk and explained that people only feel truly connected to one another when they are able to let their guard down. If they feel they must keep up appearances or do whatever they can to avoid criticism, that all-important synergy between two people—or within a group—will never happen.

As a leader, do you want a team of individuals disconnected from one another? No. Do you want a company comprised of employees who may be physically present to one another, but are mentally, psychologically, and emotionally isolated? Absolutely not. If you were a coach instead of an executive, your team might not win a single game—certainly it wouldn't win a championship. No, the most successful teams have members that are intimately connected. As Brown puts it, "There is no intimacy without vulnerability."

Exercising vulnerability—in this case, being transparent and admitting your own faults and failures—really accomplishes three things:

## 1. Vulnerability disarms people.

All too often, people come to a meeting ready for a fight. They are defensive and, as we all know, people on the defensive often get offensive. Worried that they will be criticized, their inward posture becomes what karate masters call a "fighting horse stance."

But what if, instead of swinging reverse punches at others, you took a few self-inflicted wounds? How would that change the dynamic in the office? I'll tell you how: when you admit fault, confess failure, even poke fun and laugh at yourself and your screw-ups, your people will know that your first priority is taking responsibility and holding yourself accountable, not finding scapegoats and passing on the blame. The atmosphere will change from combative to communal. You won't be adversaries playing the war game of blame, you'll be allies working together to discover solutions and get things done.

## 2. Vulnerability establishes trust.

One of my favorite videos on YouTube—one that went viral in a big way—shows a blindfolded man standing on a street corner wearing a placard that says, "Do you trust me? I trust you. Free Hugs." Yes, that's right. He just stands there and holds out his arms, waiting for the first person to embrace. At first, no one takes him up on the offer. But slowly, surely, one woman hugs him, then a man, then a couple more women and men, until eventually there is a throng of people who, one by one, embrace the man. It's pretty moving, really. It touches a deep emotional chord when you watch it. That's why, at last check, it had almost half a million views.

> When we take risks and are vulnerable, even in the basic admission of a mistake, we establish trust.

The moving scenes depicted in this video could not have happened if the man hadn't taken a risk. Think about it: he was blindfolded. People could have taunted him (maybe they did) and he wouldn't have known who said what. Worse, who's to say somebody wouldn't have walked up and sucker punched him? Putting these possibilities aside, he put himself out there. He took a risk and established trust. Because of that, he brightened the day of a lot of people.

It's the same way with leadership. When we take risks and are vulnerable, even in the basic admission of a mistake, we establish trust. Trust is the building block for any relationship—including a working relationship.


## 3. Vulnerability inspires others to be real.

When a leader is willing to open up and be honest and transparent about faults and failures, other members of the team and company will follow suit. Being real begets others to be real. Bank on it.

Vulnerability and honesty create the kind of dynamic environment that leads to success. Guess what you get when you have a group of people being honest about their weaknesses and failures, establishing trust with one another, connecting on an (appropriately) intimate level, and feeling the freedom to be bold and share new and exciting ideas without the fear of cruelty or criticism? You have one hell of a great work environment that will, almost certainly, be an incubator for success—and lots of it.

## Give It to Them Straight When They Screw Up

There's a flip side of that transparency thing. If a leader is going to be open and honest about his mistakes, he can (and should) hold others accountable for theirs. I know that it is very popular to promote the "sandwich method" of motivation: giving feedback about a mistake by making three statements—positive, negative, positive. Something like:

*Positive: Hey, we really value you and you perform well.*

*Negative: You're treating your staff poorly.*

*Positive: You have a great singing voice and we love you.*

Although the intent is a good one—to make the person feel valued—I actually think that you're subtly devaluing the person by doing this. First, you're putting the focus on your employee's feelings rather than the issue. If an employee comes out of a meeting feeling good about himself but misses the point, then he won't do what is required. If he doesn't do what is required, he may get fired, which will most likely cancel out any positive feelings he had about himself. Second, it assumes that your employee won't have the strength to take the truth or, worse, makes your employee assume that you don't think he's worth the truth. Third, it's just a bit disingenuous. Your point in meeting with this employee is to deal with a negative issue. It's not to tell him what a great job he is doing and how he is so wonderful and then to mention, "Oh and by the way, if you don't stop this, you and your wonderful personality and value will be out of a job." It smacks of fakeness.

## Try Accountability, Then Affirmation

Instead, I believe in accountability followed by affirmation.

*Accountability: John, I've heard you verbally abusing your staff. Your actions are straining relationships and affecting the productivity of your entire department. If you do not stop, there will be consequences.*

*Affirmation: Now, I want you to know I hope you turn things around. Because I want you to succeed. You bring great knowledge and skills to your position. You have positively contributed to this company. I'm rooting for you!*

The benefit of this is that you give equal importance to two things: truth and love. I'd like to say I came up with this myself, but I didn't. The concept is part of the moral teaching of several religious traditions, but is also common sense, isn't it?

The point is that you aren't really loving someone if you aren't willing to tell them the truth. Conversely, people are more likely to listen to the truth if it comes from someone they believe genuinely cares about them.

Bottom line: It's not an either/or. It's a both/and. In real love, you communicate the truth—and if you leave it out, your message will be lost.

## Care Enough to Show Anger

> I think there is this idea that getting angry with someone is somehow not kind, not big-hearted. That's baloney.

I also hold people accountable to expectations. I care enough to show real anger if things are not done—and done right. If I asked for a report two times and I didn't get it, I let people know very strongly that this is not acceptable. And I don't care if it is in a meeting or in front of a group of people. I say, "Why haven't I been given this? What's the problem?" I think there is this idea that getting angry with someone is somehow not kind, not big-hearted. That's baloney. Getting angry is part of being real. It says that you honor someone enough to give him or her real responsibilities because you have high expectations of them. Your anger shows that you know that person has high potential—potential that isn't being reached—and he or she matters enough to be pushed to hit that potential.

It is often assumed that showing anger means that you are a jerk and that you're being mean to your employees. Hardly. If a mother catches her child stealing, what would we think if she wasn't bothered at all? That she doesn't love him? Of course not; if she gets angry it's because she is worried about him. In the same way, anger shows that you care. You care that the person is not succeeding and you care about the success of the company. If you didn't care, you would simply let him or her go.

Of course, it would be easy to let anger degenerate into insults and personal attacks. I'm not suggesting you let that happen. I don't think you should say, "You didn't do this for me? You're such a stupid loser!" No, focus on the problem, not the person, as they always say. Keep your anger trained at the poor performance, not the personnel. Separate the act from the employee. But, for goodness sake, don't be the executive equivalent of an overindulgent helicopter parent.

Underachievers might not make the cut, but your best and brightest will work harder to be a cut above the rest.

## Exercise the Freedom to Show Affection

Affection is vital to Big-Hearted Leadership. And here's the key: the reason that you're going to be able to hold people accountable and express anger is that, hopefully, it happens rarely. The general rule is affection—appropriate affection. For me, appropriate affection is comprised of three things: hoorays, hugs, and humor.

## 1. Hoorays

The best way to show your affection is simply to praise your employees. Do it a lot. Celebrate their successes. When things go well, make sure they know. "It's because of you guys! You did this! Great job!" Like I said, if they know that you are the kind of leader who will hold people accountable and care enough to get angry, they will know that your praise is not hollow. It is not just warm, fuzzy, and empty rhetoric. They know you mean it, because if they didn't do a good job, you would say so!

## 2. Hugs

I am a hugger. That said, I completely understand that not everybody likes someone to invade his or her personal space. I also understand that things can get confused, misunderstood, and misinterpreted. That's why I will repeat something I wrote earlier: a Big-Hearted Leader should know his or her people well enough to instinctively know whether a hug is okay. He or she will also have built enough trust to know whether physical affection—a hug, a pat on the back, whatever—will be okay. To paraphrase Tommy Callahan, "[Leaders] don't shake hands. [Leaders] gotta hug!"

## 3. Humor

I think humor is an indispensable form of affection. I don't think humor implies that a leader is soft or not serious about the job. Growing up in Minnesota in the 1970s, I was a huge Vikings fan and admired the now-legendary hall of fame coach Bud Grant. No one could accuse that guy of not being tough as nails. He was legendary for his stone face. He was an old-school disciplinarian. And sometimes, during games, he'd wear short sleeves in the frigid Minnesota winter. It was a subtle reminder to the opposing team that his team was tough and that his team scoffed at the freezing temperatures. "There is a time and place for everything," he said. "But the sideline is not the place for yuks."

If you know anything about Bud Grant, you also know that he could be a barrel of laughs. I remember an article in the *Pittsburgh Press* in December of 1976 that talked about all his antics. He un-caged a rooster in the women's bathroom at his office one April Fool's Day. He drenched sleeping players with wastebaskets full of cold water. He developed the goofy pre-game ritual of eating an ice cream sundae with a reporter friend, Ralph Reeve, before every game. He was a serious man with a serious sense of humor.

A Big-Hearted Leader knows that humor is a way that you bond with people. Laughing is one of the greatest shared experiences of humankind. It can also be a huge stress reliever, one that takes the edge off a situation that requires calm.

One of the main ways that I use humor in leadership is by giving nicknames. Everybody gets a nickname. It's endearing. It builds familiarity. And it implies a mutual level of respect. The truth is, who kids around with someone they hate? Exactly—no one.

Do what you can to season the day with a little humor. Small pranks. Poking fun. Exercise your own personal humor in meetings, speeches, and presentations. And don't tell me you don't have a sense of humor. We're all born with one. So be optimistic that you can make your team smile and chuckle. In fact, adopt the attitude of Lloyd Christmas from *Dumb and Dumber*. If that little voice of insecurity inside you says, *You've got about a one in a million chance to make people laugh*, just respond, *So you're telling me there's a chance!*

> Do what you can to season the day with a little humor.

Sometimes a sense of humor just has to be exercised and developed. Find out what works for you. And you know what? Even having an unusual sense of humor—a dry or quirky one—can be endearing. The key is to be real and honest.

\* \* \*

At the beginning of this chapter, I wrote that we live in an age where leaders can face overwhelming scrutiny and often respond by doing everything they can to adjust to the demands of the crowd. The truth is, there have been some developments in our culture that should make any leader smile. Yes, anyone who is in a leadership position and is consistently out in front of people will continue to be subject to (often unfair and unrealistic) expectations and standards. Leaders are just people, after all. On the other hand, our culture as a whole appears to have grown extremely tired of anything that is too pretentious or over-produced. What are the most viewed programs on television these days? Reality shows. Who are the most wildly popular personalities with the largest social media followings? More often than not, it's the athletes, actors, executives, politicians, and others who communicate in largely unfiltered ways and who adopt a "take me as I am" disposition. Now, am I suggesting you take all your cues from Gary Vaynerchuk or Kim Kardashian? With regard to the former, maybe some. With regard to the latter . . . well, that's your call! What I am suggesting is that there is—and will increasingly be—a direct connection between your success as a leader and your willingness to be the real you. The titan of influence herself, Oprah Winfrey, once said: "I had no idea that being your authentic self could make me as rich as I've become. If I had, I'd have done it a lot earlier." In the same way, I think you may have no idea how successful you can be as a leader just by being your authentic self. It does take courage. It does take vulnerability. But I honestly think you will be rewarded. I've experienced those rewards myself.

Trust me: there's power in being yourself. And it's a whole lot easier than trying to be someone else.

# CHAPTER FOUR:
## Possess (and Pass On) Enduring Enthusiasm

---

*"Pleasure in the job puts perfection
in the work."*

**ARISTOTLE**

---

I AM A BLESSED MAN FOR A NUMBER OF REASONS. One thing I am particularly grateful for is that, on the average day, I don't need an alarm clock. I'm excited enough about getting to work that I beat the "beep beep" to the punch.

Now I don't want to make it sound like my job is all rainbows and unicorns and happy hours. Like any position, mine comes with stresses and downsides.

Every now and then, there are bad moments, bad meetings, bad days, maybe even bad weeks.

But you know what? If hard pressed, I honestly couldn't tell you much about the bad stuff because I don't make a point to remember it. Seriously. And even if there is a period of time when there are more lows than highs, it doesn't dim my spirit or dent my attitude because the daily good at work far outweighs the occasional bad. I love my job and I have an enduring enthusiasm for it.

Enduring enthusiasm is an essential quality of a Big-Hearted Leader. That's because enthusiasm is so critical for success, both in life and business. Just ask the experts—poets, politicians, entrepreneurs, self-help gurus, or bartenders—they all agree:

- Ralph Waldo Emerson said, "Nothing great was ever achieved without enthusiasm."

- Winston Churchill said, "Success consists of going from failure to failure without loss of enthusiasm."

- Henry Ford said, "Enthusiasm is the yeast that makes your hopes shine to the stars. Enthusiasm is the sparkle in your eyes, the swing in your gait. The grip of your hand, the irresistible surge of will and energy to execute your ideas."

- And Dale Carnegie said, "Flaming enthusiasm, backed up by horse sense and persistence, is the quality that most frequently makes for success."

Is enthusiasm important and necessary to lead an organization? Absolutely. There are two main reasons why:

1. People are human and have finite levels of energy. There's a natural tendency for us to get tired and discouraged. It's the second law of thermodynamics—as we work, our energy diminishes. Enthusiasm is necessary to sustain and recharge energy.

2. People lose focus. When enthusiasm wanes, sometimes our focus blurs, too. We aren't excited about what we're doing so we actually lose sight of what it is we're supposed to be doing. This is when we can experience mission creep. The focus shifts and failure is sure to follow. Enthusiasm keeps us focused.

Because enthusiasm is so important, I want to take a moment to further explain exactly what I mean when I use the word. Sure, there's the dictionary definition: "Intense and eager enjoyment, interest, or approval," but I want to go deeper than that.

As I've mentioned, I serve a nationally ranked Catholic healthcare system, so the identity of the organization includes a strong religious, or spiritual, component. Interestingly, the original meaning of the word "enthusiasm" also has a religious component. The word is rooted in the Greek language and literally means "the god" (entheos) "inside" (iasm). Originally, it meant that a person was "inhabited by the spirit of God."

You know what? Sometimes at work I do feel "inhabited by the spirit of God." It feels pretty great. You don't have to be religious to get what I'm saying here. Just exercise your imagination a bit. If you felt directly connected to the elements of the universe—the blazing sun, the beautiful mountains, all the raw materials that became Busch Stadium (sorry, I'm a Cards fan!)—it would make you happy. Plus, you'd feel cosmic strength pulsing through your body, so you'd feel supremely capable—like there's nothing you couldn't accomplish.

Now let's apply that to work: When are you enthusiastic about your job? When it makes you happy and you feel capable of doing it well. When you feel—dare I say it—almost "god-like." And here's the thing: if you are going to be successful, you have to feel that way about your job and the company or organization you lead. And you have to be able to transfer that feeling to those you lead.

I'll say it again: you have to possess that kind of enduring enthusiasm, and you have to know how to pass it on to others.

## Start with the One in the Mirror

Remember the man in the mirror that Michael Jackson famously sang about? To be more inclusive, I say that you should start with "the one" in the mirror. As a leader, you're the very first person who has to possess enduring enthusiasm. Why? According to social scientists Nicholas Christakis and James Fowler in their book *Connected: The Surprising Power of Our Social Networks and How They Shape Our Lives*, human beings are hardwired for social influence and our emotions are transmitted rapidly from person to person. In *The Face-to-Face Book*, Ed Keller and Brad Fay sum it up this way: "Everything about us is contagious." That means that people will "catch" things from you, whether you're consciously trying to exert an influence or not. You will either "infect" people with your boredom and negativity or your excitement and joy.

> You will either "infect" people with your boredom and negativity or your excitement and joy.

So what's the verdict? Are you generally and consistently enthusiastic about your job and the company you lead? You probably shouldn't have to think too hard about this. Either you are or you aren't. For the sake of helping you think it through, here are seven questions to ask yourself, to determine whether or not you are an authentic example of enthusiasm:

## 1. Do you believe in the product or service your company or organization offers?

It's not difficult for me to be excited about the organization I serve. Originally a ministry founded in Ireland by Sister Catherine McAuley, Mercy Health is in the business of changing lives—or, in many cases, saving them. Our tagline is "Your life is our life's work." That's awesome, isn't it? That's actually how I try to approach my own position and all the work I do in it— from reporting to a board of directors to writing this book, *your* life is my life's work. My enthusiasm is never in short supply.

Now, I realize that not every organization is in the business of *literally* saving lives, but that doesn't mean that whatever products or services your company provides aren't extremely worthwhile. Whether you are the head of a nonprofit organization responsible for rescuing baby seals or the CEO of a company that manufactures perforated metal, your work matters and you always have the choice to embrace that truth with enthusiasm. But here's the key: if deep in your heart you don't think your company is doing something worthwhile, then you're in trouble.

## 2. Do you believe in the integrity of the company you serve?

There are a lot of companies that offer great products or services. They might make the best coffee grinders or provide the most excellent lawn care, but behind the scenes, how do they conduct business? Poor treatment of employees? Shady bookkeeping? Of course, every organization has its inconsistencies and areas for improvement. Every company has some sour or rotten apples in an otherwise fruitful orchard. But are you generally confident in the character of your company? Of course, as a leader you have a huge influence on that, but sometimes there are deeply ingrained issues that are difficult for one person to change.

## 3. Do you believe in the mission or vision of the company you serve?

This question goes hand in hand with the first question, as the mission of an organization dovetails with the products or services it offers. But mission or vision often refers to how you want your product or service to impact the world. Think about the change the organization you serve is trying to accomplish. Do you recognize the need for that change? Do you want to be an accomplice to that change? If not—danger!

Lack of real belief in your mission or vision is not just dangerous for you. The real threat isn't that you'll be miserable at your job. The threat goes way beyond your emotional health and satisfaction as a leader. If you don't really believe in the mission or vision of the company you serve, who will suffer? Your people. The team that you direct. In the Bible, King Solomon, who, according to legend, was the wisest man in history, wrote, "Where there is no vision, the people perish" (Proverbs 29:18).

It's easy to see why. A leader who doesn't see the value in the enterprise that he or she is leading? That's an oxymoron. Or maybe just a moron. Either way, asking people to follow that person is just plain cruel.

## 4. Do you agree with the company's core values and/or social values?

Today, it is especially common for companies to trumpet some sort of social value such as service to the poor, racial diversity, you name it. I think that's a good thing. Large organizations ought to use their power and resources to influence the world for good. But facts are facts: not everybody agrees on hot-button social issues. If you serve a company that works hard to advance something that you personally disagree with, are you going to be enthusiastic about being a leader in that company? I'll answer that question for you: nope.

## 5. Do you possess the right disposition for leadership?

This might be a strange question to ask in a book about leadership. I mean, if you're reading this, doesn't it mean you want to be (or already are) a leader and have the disposition for it? Not necessarily. I've been around long enough to know that sometimes able and intelligent people fall into leadership positions because of their family background or social connections. There are a lot of wonderful, intelligent people who, deep down, simply don't want to be a leader—it isn't in their DNA. If that's you, don't feel bad about it. Be who you are. However, if this is the case, maintaining enthusiasm for your job is going to be a Herculean task. My advice: 1) Consider all the people who are dependent on you for financial support—like a spouse or children. 2) Develop a plan to transition out of your leadership position that gives you time to adjust to the change in income. (Let's face it: moving out of a leadership position into a lower-level position will probably mean a reduction in salary.) 3) Once you are certain you can meet your financial obligations, make the move as soon as possible. Putting it off won't do you or anyone else any good. On the other hand, when you are happy with your position, that happiness will transfer to those around you.

## 6. Are you in the right seat on the bus?

This question is very closely related to the last one. Maybe you do want to be *a* leader in a company or organization, but not *the* leader. Or maybe you want to be a leader in the marketing department, but the company has put you in accounting. As the saying goes, "You're in the wrong seat on the bus." Is this your situation? Well, "playing out of position" can be frustrating for the most gifted athlete, and it will definitely be frustrating for you. So, if possible, get up and move.

## 7. Are you generally energized by the work?

A couple years ago, the entrepreneur and marketing guru Seth Godin was on vacation in some tropical location, and he took a few moments to take care of a few business matters. He overheard a guy nearby say, "Man, I feel sorry for a guy who has to do work on his vacation." Seth's response was great: "I feel sorry for the guy who doesn't enjoy doing his work on his vacation." I completely agree with him. I've never understood the people who "live for the whistle and the weekend." Nobody should be a workaholic, but if it's within your power (and for most people, it is), you should work at a job you enjoy—and working at that job should energize you.

If you answered "yes" to all these questions, there's no reason you shouldn't be enduringly and wildly enthusiastic about your job. If you answered "no" to any of them, you should be able to determine whether the issue can be addressed and fixed. If it can't, or if you answered "no" to most or all of these questions, then I've got news for you: You need to quit. Change jobs. Move on.

This may not be financially viable for you to do right away, but you should do it as soon as possible. I believe with all my heart that you cannot be an effective leader if you aren't enthusiastic about your job or the organization you lead. At the end of the day, a leader— especially a Big-Hearted Leader—is like a fountain. There has to be a gush from the center of your heart and soul that overflows to fill up the hearts and minds of those you lead. That's the only way you're going to naturally and consistently transfer enduring enthusiasm to your people.

So, if you're not enthusiastic, make whatever changes you need to make—even if they are radical changes. If you are enthusiastic, you may still not know the best, most strategic ways to transfer that enthusiasm to your people. That's the subject of the next section. In fact, I'm going to talk about what to be enthusiastic about, whom to transfer the enthusiasm to, and how to transfer the enthusiasm.

## What to Be Enthusiastic About

So what should you be enthusiastic about in the scheme of Big-Hearted Leadership?

First, be enthusiastic about the main mission of the company. You constantly hold the big picture before your people. You point the flag at what you are trying to accomplish and you tie everything into that.

> You constantly hold the big picture before your people.

Second, be enthusiastic about the core values and goals of the company. I always choose three to five core values or goals to focus on at the organizations I serve. I want people to know them cold—to have them memorized. At any given time, if I ask you, "What are our goals?" you should be able to say, "Customer satisfaction. Patient care. Bottom line."

Third, be enthusiastic about the fact that achieving these core values is not an either/or but a both/and. If you are trying to improve provider satisfaction, you don't want patient care to suffer. It's not about choosing options—the point is to fulfill all the core values. Take the opportunity to get people enthusiastic about the fact that it can be done.

But also know that there's a dynamic balance

involved. Notice that I didn't say "delicate balance." Using the term "delicate" implies too much finality; as if you achieve a balance and hope that it doesn't break. The better phrase is "dynamic balance." As in, the opposite of static. You have to realize that your emphasis and attention to different core values will be fluid. There will be moments in the life of your organization when one core value *temporarily* moves to the forefront. That's okay. The key is to not so constantly emphasize that core value at the expense of the others that it's like you're trying to fly a plane with only one wing. You will need to give attention to all of your core values at different times in order to soar.

Fourth, be enthusiastic about successes—your employees' successes. I can't stress this enough. You have to constantly show people when they are successful, and you need to tell them, "You did that! You guys did that!" In his book *Influence*, Robert B. Cialdini explains that people have a limitless capacity for praise. Compliments will influence how they think of you. They will feel better about themselves and they will like you more. There will be a real heart connection. A big-hearted connection.

## To whom do you transfer enthusiasm?

The short answer is everybody.

Transfer enthusiasm to yourself. We've already talked about that. You're not transferring enthusiasm as much as appropriating it.

Transfer enthusiasm to your board. These are the men and women who, in theory, are most fully invested in your organization. If your board is bored, you can bet the spirit of "So what?" will spread throughout your organization. So, it's important that the people on the top are kept "sold" on the vision and mission of the organization—and the goals.

> Transfer enthusiasm to every employee that you meet.

Transfer enthusiasm to your mid-level management (and encourage them to transfer it to their staff). This is a huge constituency that can't be overlooked. In most cases, the boots-on-the-ground employee will not have regular, direct interaction with upper-level management. There's a disconnect there that makes it difficult to transfer enthusiasm. So make sure that when you transfer enthusiasm to your mid-level employees, they see themselves not as reservoirs, but as conduits.

We don't want people to simply fill up on enthusiasm. We want them to pass it on.

Transfer enthusiasm to every employee that you meet. When you are walking down a hall, in casual conversation, wherever you go, transfer enthusiasm. Everyone at every level should be a target for transfer.

Transfer enthusiasm to the media. You want good PR, so you should constantly be talking to people in the press, regardless of your level of access. If you're a small-business owner, you can cultivate relationships with local reporters, writers, bloggers, and industry publications. If you are the president of a major organization, you'll have access—maybe more than you want—to reporters and talk show hosts and the like. Take every opportunity you can to sell the people in the media on the mission and goals and accomplishments of your organization.

Transfer enthusiasm to the community. Form relationships with key people in your community who aren't necessarily media outlets. Make appearances and speak at local civic groups about the vision, mission, and goals of your organization. In almost every case, the people of the local community are the direct beneficiaries of the success of your business. From the way your business contributes to the economy to the support it provides for any number of civic or social programs, you should actively show people how enthusiastic you are about serving them. In turn, you want them to get enthusiastic about being served. Pass on the passion to every kind of local leader and influencer you can think of—from the police chief and fire marshal to the attorney general to the archbishop. Form a vast network of enthusiastic community supporters. Trust me: that enthusiasm is some of the best capital you can raise. Practical benefits for your business will abound.

## How to Transfer Enthusiasm

First, transfer enthusiasm in small conversations. Conversation is the currency of leadership and influence. It's as simple as that.

Second, sell enthusiasm through stories and anecdotes. Stats and facts are important, but they're not always inspiring. Sell people on the vision and mission of your organization by showing how the organization impacted someone's life. Believe me, whether you are head of a health system or a plumbing company, you can find a way to show how your work impacts people.

Third, transfer enthusiasm by specifically naming people who were part of a particular example of success.

It's always important to give credit and recognition. The more you do that, the more people will connect with you—and the more enthused they will be about giving extra effort in the future.

Fourth, when you transfer enthusiasm, make connections. Help employees to see that what they did specifically resulted in something good. Don't just say, "We accomplished this," but, "We accomplished this because John did X, and Sally did Y, and Tom did Z." Show them the direct results of their actions.

Fifth, transfer enthusiasm with large group presentations. There should definitely be times you get out the microphone and PowerPoint and officially deliver a presentation to your staff or entire company. Don't be afraid of public speaking. Just be yourself.

Sixth, you'll want to transfer enthusiasm through interoffice emails and in-house newsletters. Mercy, like most other organizations, has newsletters that regularly celebrate successes and/or identify people who are doing their jobs well and accomplishing great things. Email marketing and communications are so inexpensive these days, there's no reason to not tap into their powers of communication.

## Let's End with an Ancient Story

Not long ago, I came across an ancient story that really got me jacked up. The story goes like this:

Once upon a time, there was a powerful and oppressive ruler who commanded an army of tens of thousands. He was opposed by a young, valiant prince who led a group of noble soldiers that barely numbered a thousand. The oppressive ruler sent a messenger to the young prince, warning him to surrender or be destroyed. After the messenger delivered the message, the young prince called one of his soldiers over to where they were standing.

He said to his soldier, "Plunge your knife into your heart!"

The soldier took his knife and plunged it into his own heart.

The messenger was astonished, but the young prince called another soldier over to him.

He pointed to a nearby cliff with a steep, deadly drop off.

"Throw yourself off of yonder cliff," the prince said to his soldier.

Without hesitating, the soldier ran to the edge of the cliff and jumped off.

The young prince turned to the messenger.

"I have nearly a thousand soldiers, each one like those two men," he said. "Our blood flows with passion. We believe in our cause. We will die, but we will never surrender."

Then the young prince looked the messenger dead in the eye.

"You tell that oppressive ruler that we will pursue him in battle," he said. "And by the end of this week, he will be chained at my feet with my dog."

The messenger hurried away and returned to the oppressive ruler. A cowardly bully at heart, the ruler was terrified and ordered a full retreat, attempting to flee the valiant young prince and his passionate warriors.

He did not succeed. The two armies met in battle. By the end of the week, the oppressive ruler was chained at the young prince's feet—next to his dog.

While I don't advocate asking your team members to stab themselves or jump off cliffs, nor do I think chaining someone at your feet like a dog is a good idea, this is the kind of enthusiasm that you want in your people and for your company. If you don't have it, neither will they.

For me, this goes beyond exercising good leadership

to helping your people enjoy a good life. When leaders are enthusiastic, that enthusiasm—as I have said—is transferred to others. Through that transfer, emotional bonds are formed. When emotional bonds are formed, people become fiercely loyal to one another. Have you ever been on a team characterized by a genuine, heartfelt *affection* for one another? It's an incredible experience. C.S. Lewis, the author of those great children's books *The Chronicles of Narnia,* once wrote that "affection is responsible for nine-tenths of whatever solid and durable happiness there is in our lives." I agree with him. Transferring enthusiasm to your people is a starting point for enhancing and elevating not just your effectiveness, but their happiness.

# CHAPTER FIVE:
## Turn Your Organization into a Force for Good

---

*"Mankind was my business. The common welfare was my business; charity, mercy, forbearance, benevolence, were all my business. The dealings of my trade were but a drop of water in the comprehensive ocean of my business!"*

**MARLEY'S GHOST, *A CHRISTMAS CAROL* BY Charles Dickens**

---

IN 2005, I STEPPED INTO A KITCHEN AND WAS NEVER the same again. At the time, I was serving as COO of Mercy Health in Springfield, Missouri. It was early

December, and by virtue of my position as a leader in the community, I was asked to help a local nonprofit that provided a hotel, resource center, and doctor's office for the homeless. It was called the Kitchen.

Shortly after I arrived, I was stunned. The Kitchen provides housing and stabilizing services to those who don't have a place to sleep, don't have food to eat, don't have the means to tend to their health, and are barely making it.

What impacted me about that visit was just looking around and seeing so many people—quality people—who were living with challenges and in conditions that I couldn't even wrap my head around. Some were old enough to be my grandparents; others were young enough to be my kids. I kept shaking my head and thinking, *Are you kidding me? This is real. Good people are really living this way.*

I'm not sure why I was so shocked. I grew up with the blessings of a financially stable household—food, shelter, clothing, and more—but was certainly not born with a silver spoon in my mouth or spoiled throughout my upbringing. I wasn't sheltered, either. I had friends from all sorts of socioeconomic backgrounds. In theory, at least, I grew up knowing that the United States has its poor and homeless. But I didn't experience either up close, so they remained an abstract concept. The very real problems of homelessness and poverty didn't seem very real to me.

Now, it wasn't like I was Ebenezer Scrooge from *A Christmas Carol*, who actively and intentionally dismissed the needs of others. I wasn't looking at the poor and saying "Bah! Humbug! I don't need to help you." But that's no excuse—it's very bad to refuse to help a person in need, but it's also bad to be so clueless that you neglect to help them. By and large, that's what I was guilty of for a large part of my career.

My trip to the Kitchen changed that. When I got back to the office that day, we had an all-manager meeting. I called everybody together and said, "Listen, there's a real problem right here in our community, and we need to do something about it. There's a wrong that needs to be righted, and we're a big organization with the influence and resources to help right that wrong." We decided to raise money and help in whatever way we could. In the next two weeks, we raised over $50,000 and—as it was the month of December—gave away bags and bags of toys. It was one small but meaningful step toward trying to right a wrong in our society. And frankly, it felt darn good.

We created an ongoing program that I called Force

for Good, a charitable entity within the Mercy Health System that encourages employees to pick a charity and then get involved in volunteering, fundraising, and donating. It's not corporate giving—although that happens at Mercy, too. It's physicians and managers and other employees coming together and creating their own fundraisers—from bake sales to silent auctions. Force for Good means direct personal involvement and an investment of their time, talent, and treasure.

> There's nothing that a Big-Hearted Leader can do that is more important than turning his or her company or organization into a force for good.

In my opinion, there's nothing that a Big-Hearted Leader can do that is more important than turning his or her company or organization into a force for good.

## Business Leaders Are Best Suited to Help

As the Big-Hearted Leader, you have a unique opportunity to position your company as a force for good, since businesspeople are in a uniquely advantageous position to help others in need. How so?

**Business leaders are generally good at making**

**money.** Whether you're the leader of a small business or large corporation, at a very basic level, the purpose of a business is to make money. As such, the average businessperson, by the very nature of business, has usually discovered skills that assist in that quest—whether organizational skills or marketing acumen. Good businesspeople are good at making money. So it makes sense that you might be good at making money to support a great cause.

**Leaders of all businesses tend to be well connected.** We live in a very social world, and it's easier than ever to be connected. But as a business leader, it's almost a necessity to be extremely well connected. And you tend to be well connected with other successful people who have the financial resources and means to advance a cause with significant results. Being well connected is vitally important. There is a lot of wrong in this world that needs to be made right. You're not going to right things all by yourself. Many people are in need. It will take many people to help them.

**Individual business leaders benefit from an organization's reputation.** Bolstered by their organization's reputation, business leaders can bring a sense of authority and gravitas to a particular cause and help motivate the average person on the street to get involved and to support the cause. Just think about it: what if you heard that Donn Sorensen is the official sponsor of Care to Learn? Care to Learn is a charity I help lead that provides immediate funding to meet emergent health, hunger, and hygiene needs so every child can be successful in school (learn more at caretolearnfund.org). You may think, *So what?* But if you heard that I'm with Mercy Health, that's when my involvement carries more weight. Mercy is a trusted organization in the community; as an entity, it is far more impressive than the individuals working for it. People are more likely to support a cause if a trusted company name is attached to it.

## The Benefits Are Both Personal and Professional

A guy known as Jesus of Nazareth once said, "Be innocent as doves, but shrewd as serpents" (Matthew 10:16). I'm no biblical scholar, but I understand the Jewish carpenter to be saying that character and cunning aren't necessarily opposed to one another. You can be a good person who does good things—things that, as a nice little cherry on top, also make good business sense. Well, that's definitely the case for Big-Hearted Leaders who turn their businesses into a force for good. There are both personal and professional benefits.

**First, you'll feel like a superhero.** Seriously—it feels damn good to help out people in need. Sometimes, in the midst of business, things can get a little tedious. Amid spreadsheets and customer surveys and marketing reports, it's easy to get bogged down and forget that there are bigger things going on in life than just making money and dominating market share. None of those things are bad, but at the end of the day, most people don't experience a sense of deep meaning and significance in life because of market share. When you invest time, energy, and resources into helping others out and making the world a better place, you actually end up helping yourself. Your life is imbued with meaning and, like I said, that feels damn good.

> It's easy to get bogged down and forget that there are bigger things going on in life than just making money and dominating market share.

If you don't think adding meaning improves employee satisfaction, you're missing something. It's one thing to come to work and be part of a great company or project. That's enough to make you feel all right. But if your employees are able to link their work to a great cause that helps others, they will feel exponentially better about themselves. Satisfied and happy employees are generally productive employees. Delight translates to dollars.

**Second, you'll be more grateful.** When you are helping others meet their basic needs, like being clothed, fed, and sheltered, it puts your wants and needs into perspective. Are you still going to complain because your desk could be bigger? Are you still going to be upset because the return on your investment wasn't as great as it could have been? Probably not. Work with people who are suffering and have nothing—or close to nothing— and suddenly life looks pretty good. Complaints get silenced.

In the same way, if you have a bunch of employees working to help those in need, they can't help being affected by it. Employees are much less likely to grumble or complain or be petty about their disappointments with their bosses or jobs when other people's stark lives are held up in front of them. Once again, it will bring perspective to your company and silence—or at least lower the volume—on the chronic complainers. It does nothing but good for your company.

**Third, you give your employees the chance to change the lives of others.** Let's say you host a fundraiser and you raise $25,000 to keep a food bank well-stocked for months. People feel like they have contributed to and accomplished something that is making a real, tangible difference in others' lives. If employees feel that success, if they know that they can contribute to the success of something so life changing, it will give them confidence to accomplish other things. They will think, *If we can do that, what's to stop us from handling improvements to our manufacturing processes? Let's put our heads together and do it!* That sense of accomplishment is transferable.

In addition to these personal and professional benefits, there are a couple of other benefits that are no-brainers. The local community loves it when a business invests in the needs of others—so it's a public relations plus. Oftentimes, charities have multiple sponsors, so it's an opportunity to strengthen business-to-business relationships and network with other professionals.

## Take Action

So, here's the bottom line: use your business as a force for good. There are two ways to do that:

### 1. Get your business involved with an already-existing charity.

There are so many worthwhile charities already in existence, so you don't have to start your own. In addition to good-old Google, you can use specialized cause search engines like Guidestar.org or CharityNavigator. org to research those charitable causes that really interest you. Find one that promotes a cause or meets a need that you really resonate with. Find out how they do things and determine whether a synergy and like-mindedness exists between the nonprofit and your business. Find out whether there are good opportunities locally—not just to get involved and support, but to lead. Above all, find out if the nonprofit is a good fit. If it is, forge a relationship and use all your local resources and manpower as a force for good.

### 2. Start your own nonprofit.

There are many worthwhile causes out there, and I do not think it's usually necessary to start your own nonprofit. However, in some cases, there may be organizations that help meet a need you care about, but not in the way you would do it. Or there might be organizations addressing a particular need, but not enough of them. If that's the case, go ahead and start a nonprofit.

I will tell you this—if you want to succeed at starting your own nonprofit, you'll need three things:

**A mission statement.** First, you'll want to have a clearly defined mission statement and revisit it often so you don't have "mission creep"—which is a mission that grows and migrates and becomes so large that it loses its focus. It's difficult to stay on track sometimes, because charity work is hard work. You need to know exactly what your mission is at all times.

**Well-known supporters.** You need people with visibility to get behind your charity. I'm blessed to have awesome friends like NHL great Brett Hull, prominent broadcaster Joe Buck, and NFL legend Isaac Bruce putting their names behind Care to Learn. And that's good because people are not going to come to a fundraiser and give just because Donn Sorensen is there. In the public's eyes, I don't possess enough star power. On the other hand, people want to be associated with things that are associated with people they hold in high esteem. In our society, more often than not, those types of people are athletes, actors, and other celebrities. I envision a bright, sparkling future world where healthcare executives will be celebrities! But since that's not going to happen anytime soon, I needed to bring in the star power—in this case, people in sports and broadcasting—to get people excited enough to invest their funds.

**Fundraisers.** While we're on the subject of funds, you better figure out how to host a fundraiser—because they are the lifeblood of all successful charities. I recommend starting small and working your way up to a major gala event. I've learned from others who did it before me—and did it better—but you may not have that benefit. If that's the case, I do recommend using the resources of the Association of Fundraising Professionals (afpnet.org).

### 3. Forge friendships with prominent people who are forces for good.

In some ways, this is the most important thing I can tell you to do. Earlier, when I talked about starting your own nonprofit, I mentioned the need for well-known "names" to get behind your effort. The truth is, you need to go beyond simply getting people with star power to enlist in your cause. If all you want is their magnetism, you'd be guilty of using them. Instead, go beyond enlisting their influence to really engaging them as people. Get to know their passions, interests, and goals. Then find ways that your missions align. Forge meaningful friendships with the movers and shakers in society that embody these three attributes:

**A heart of caring.** Can I state the obvious? Not every public figure or popular celebrity actually cares about people. They may earn a great living from their fans and followers, but they don't necessarily value those people, except to the extent they help them earn money or stroke their ego. But there are exceptions. Keep your eyes open, ask around the social circles of the city where you live, and you'll find out who the real class acts are. It's hard to fake compassion.

**A mind for business.** Compassion is good. Compassion combined with business competency is outstanding. A lot of times, a celebrity might have a load of talent in acting or athletics, but no real business or real-world skills. If you're able to build a strong friendship with a public figure whose business savvy is equal to their benevolence—well then, my friend, you have just gained a powerful ally for accomplishing great things.

**A willingness to invest time.** People are busy. More often than not, public figures and prominent personalities are even busier. There are a lot of "names" who profess a desire to be charitably active, but simply can't (or won't) find the time. Forge friendships with the people who make the time to positively impact the world. Work with people who make helping others a priority. Again, they shouldn't be difficult to find. Look around and see who is already active in a variety of great charities for good causes.

## Find a JJK and You'll be A-OK

My very good friend Jackie Joyner-Kersee ("JJK") is a woman who models all three of the characteristics I just mentioned. Most of the world knows her for her athletic accomplishments. In addition to winning six Olympic medals (three gold, one silver, two bronze) in four consecutive Olympic games, JJK was the:

- First woman to win back-to-back gold medals in the seven-discipline event, the heptathlon;

- First woman to score 7,000 points in the heptathlon;

- First American woman to win an Olympic gold medal in the long jump;

- [Is the] current world-record holder in the heptathlon.

Even with all these accomplishments, Jackie hasn't been content to lean on her athletic laurels as the primary way that she positively impacts the world. Growing up in East St. Louis, Illinois, a city with both great poverty and crime, she experienced many challenges. But she benefitted immensely from a local community center and the support of big-hearted volunteers.

As a result, Jackie has always been determined to give back. In January 2000, she opened the Jackie Joyner-Kersee Center (JJK Center) in East St. Louis, Illinois, a safe haven for young people to learn, play, and contribute back to their community. The JJK Center provides services to thousands of families and youth in the metropolitan St. Louis area. The center is an integral part of impacting and revitalizing the East St. Louis community and its youth.

The thing is, if you asked JJK why she is so active in charitable work, why she gives so much of herself, she'll tell you, "Giving is a kind of grace." When we hear of that word, "grace," we might think of "saying grace"—a prayer—before a meal. Or we might think of the "grace" of a ballerina, her beautiful agility and coordination. But Jackie means it in the spiritual sense: "grace" as "receiving a gift from God." So, interestingly enough, she's saying that when you give *of* yourself, you give a gift *to* yourself.

I believe the same thing about turning your company or organization into a force for good. Like I mentioned earlier, your work will benefit a whole lot of people, but it will benefit you a whole lot, too. The opportunity to positively impact others will impact you and your business in ways you haven't even dreamed of.

A couple of Christmases ago, I got what I originally thought was a strange gift from one of the physicians at Mercy. It was a backpack. I thought, *A backpack? Why is he giving me a backpack?* The doctor told me to look inside, and when I did, I saw that it was full of things like nonperishable foods, medical supplies, clothes, and other things you might need to survive the wilderness. I still didn't get it.

"The backpack is full of things that would help a homeless person," he said. And he just smiled knowingly.

But about a month later, I was driving in downtown St. Louis on a bitterly cold January afternoon. I stopped at an intersection and—lo and behold—I saw a homeless man sitting just off the road. He was shivering.

Truth to tell, I had ditched the backpack in my trunk. Boy, am I glad I did! I hopped out of my car real quick, popped open my trunk, and ran and gave the backpack to the gentleman on the street.

He looked at me with wide eyes, smiled, and gave me a huge, "Thank you."

All of a sudden, I understood why my physician friend's gift to me was so incredible, so priceless. It was a gift I could pass on to someone who really needed it. And the opportunity to be generous was—and is—a huge privilege. Proverbs 11:25 says, "A generous man prospers. He who refreshes others will be refreshed."

So position your company as a force for good. Professionally and personally, be generous. And don't think you're doing the world a favor. The person receiving the favor is you.

# CONCLUSION

---

*"The two most important days of your life are
the day you are born
and the day you find out why."*

**MARK TWAIN**

---

EARLIER IN THIS BOOK, I MADE A PASSING REFERENCE
to Catherine McAuley. Now as I draw to a close, I want
to tell you a little more about her.

Catherine was born in 1778 in Dublin, Ireland. By
the time she was ten, both of her parents had died and
she had become very poor and was dependent on the
charity and support of others. When she was twenty,
she became the household manager and companion for

William and Catherine Callaghan, an elderly, childless couple with substantial wealth. Twenty years later, the couple died and Catherine McAuley was shocked to discover that they had named her the sole heir of a sizable inheritance.

With that money, Catherine implemented her lifelong dream: to build a house that served as a school for poor girls and as a shelter for homeless servant girls and women. Her work and ministry continued to grow and, in September 8, 1830, Catherine entered the Presentation Convent in Dublin. One year later, she and two other women professed their vows as the first Sisters of Mercy, founding the congregation that eventually created the Mercy Health Systems, the company I serve today.

Whether you are religious or not, there are two things we can learn from Catherine that help us wrap up what it means to be a Big-Hearted Leader.

## Call It a Calling

**First, it's imperative to see your leadership position as a calling.** Throughout history, there have been people who claimed to be "called"—specially chosen and set apart—to accomplish something great (at least in their eyes or the eyes of their followers). In many cases, those names are familiar to us: Moses, Jesus, Buddha, Mohammed, Joan of Arc, Martin Luther King Jr., the list goes on.

For some very good reasons, many of us would feel gun-shy about referring to ourselves as "called." There are cult leaders who think of themselves as "called"— and they might be one fry short of a Happy Meal, crazed lunatics bent on manipulating others. Along similar lines, there are wild-eyed, gun-toting terrorists who also think of themselves as called—called to hurt and kill people.

So why on earth would I think it's helpful to think of your position as a calling? Because a calling is something that is meaningful and significant. This is no trivial pursuit you're engaged in, but an incredibly important venture. Along with that, it includes two other things necessary for Big-Hearted Leadership:

**A sense of commitment to a higher purpose.** If you haven't figured this out already, Big-Hearted Leaders believe in greater things beyond business. They believe there's more to life than money—not that cold hard cash is a bad thing. As Adam Sandler says in *The Wedding Singer*, "I'm a big fan of money. I like it. I use it." On a very literal level, the purpose of business is to make money. But many successful people—from members of the Greatest Generation to today's Millennials—have discovered that, as an enduring motivation, money doesn't cut it. Eventually, anybody motivated by money alone gets bored. That's why it's important to commit yourself to something greater, a purpose beyond earning the bucks.

This is similar to what I said about positioning your business as a force for good, but not the same. In this case, I'm not talking about your organization, but about you personally—your leadership position, and the driving force behind what you do. I'm talking about your personal mission statement. As you exercise the specific duties of your position, as you manage employees and interact with stakeholders, continually ask yourself, *What higher purpose drives all of my activities—from the decisions I make about the operating budget to the way I interact with the custodian?*

I would not presume to tell you what that purpose should be, but there are some pretty standard options that guide a large portion of the human race: ending poverty, improving society, curing illnesses, lowering crime, loving God, and others that ultimately mean helping people and making the world a better place. Pick one.

**A whole-hearted investment of your life.** I have to tread carefully here, because I don't want there to be any misunderstanding. When I talk about whole-heartedly investing your life in your position, *I am* saying that you should treat your role as a leader like it's your life. But not in the same way that workaholics treat their jobs as their lives. (And I say that as someone who definitely struggles with being a workaholic at times.) When a workaholic thinks of his or her job as life itself, it is because they have 1) granted it the status of being the most important thing, and thus 2) given it far more hours in the day and units of personal energy than is healthy. When that happens, your existence is *reduced* to your job. At the risk of contradicting myself, let me say emphatically: that's a no-no.

A better way to think of your job or position is as a vital and treasured relationship in your life. (Bear with me here, and don't accuse me of spreading cheese. This is good stuff.) You invest your life in this relationship—your role as a leader—because it makes you happy. You gain knowledge and learn exciting new things from it. Over the course of life, you experience failures and successes, victories and defeats, and you bond over the shared story, the mutual adventure. You and your role as a leader give each other the best you have. But, like any healthy relationship, you give each other space. You take time off to be alone. You have other interests and pursuits. And, more than anything else, you don't place crushing expectations on one another. You don't invest all your hopes and dreams of happiness in it. Simply put, you and your leadership position are not codependent! Your life isn't *reduced* to your job. Your position enlarges and enhances your life.

> Your life isn't *reduced* to your job. Your position enlarges and enhances your life.

## BE BOTH/AND, NOT EITHER/OR

**The second thing we can learn from Catherine McAuley is that you don't have to choose between compassion and competence.** In the introduction to this book, I tried to dispel some possible misunderstandings about Big-Hearted Leadership. This is the one I want to address one last time. Because it's huge.

McAuley was obviously compassionate. Her untiring work with the poor and underprivileged has been well documented, and there's even a growing movement in favor of her being canonized as a saint in the Catholic Church. In my opinion, that's awesome. Sometimes, however, when someone is known for having a big heart, people assume that they don't have the brains to go with it. This is a common accusation, especially of religious people whom others perceive as being on some kind of pie-in-the-sky mission of mercy to the world. Detractors say, "those people are too heavenly minded to be of any earthly good."

That was definitely not the case with Catherine McAuley. As she worked to make the world a better place, she did it with competence and cunning. She was a smart businesswoman and an able manager, and she understood very well that while money could be used for evil, it could also be used mightily for good. In a letter to Father James Maher, dated January 10, 1838, she wrote:

> *Although I should be simple as a dove,*
> *I must also be prudent as a Serpent; and since there*
> *is very little good can be accomplished or evil avoided*
> *without the aid of money, we must look after it in*
> *small as well as in great matters.*

Don't miss the point: Catherine McAuley was committed to a higher purpose *and* profoundly practical. When it came to compassion and competence, it wasn't either/or; it was both/and. The same is true of the

Big-Hearted Leader. So as you finish up this book, I hope you'll be committed to the lifelong pursuit of those two qualities.

## Tommy Callahan Has the Final Word

Well, we've come to the end. In the introduction of this book, I confessed that I love stupid movies. I'm not embarrassed by that. Not one bit. In fact, now that I've finished writing *Big-Hearted Leadership*, I think I'll celebrate by watching *Tommy Boy* one more time. I hope that you've found this book helpful. In fact, I hope you'll put a slight spin on a famous Tommy Callahan quote:

"I've [read a lot of books] in my life . . . but that . . . was . . . AWESOME!"

# About the Author

DONN SORENSEN IS A LONGTIME EXECUTIVE IN THE medical-management field and an active community and nonprofit leader. He currently serves as the president of Mercy East Region, part of the Mercy Health System, the seventh largest Catholic healthcare system in the United States. In addition, he is the board chair for the charity Care to Learn (caretolearnfund.org).

Donn is a Fellow of the American College of Medical Practice Executives and in 2016, he was elected board chair for the American Medical Group Association Board of Directors. He holds a bachelor's degree in business administration from Luther College in Decorah, Iowa; a master's in health administration from St. Mary's College in Rochester, Minnesota; and a master's in business administration from Missouri State University in Springfield, Missouri. Donn is a national speaker and has been published numerous times. He lives in St. Louis, Missouri.

Find him online at **DonnSorensen.com**.

# BIG-HEARTED LEADERSHIP

Please visit:

DonnSorensen.com *or*
Big-HeartedLeadership.com.